The BIG HEAD Diaries Volume One

The BIG HEAD Diaries Volume One

Stories of a Yellow Lab from Down Under

by
Ryan Chin

The Big Head Diaries, Volume 1

SolChin Media Group, Portland, OR
www.ryanchinauthor.com

© 2018 by Ryan Chin

All rights reserved. Published by SolChin Media Group. No part of this publication may be reproduced or distributed in any form or by any means, or stored in a database or retrieval system, without the prior written permission of the publisher.

Editing and design by Indigo: Editing, Design, and More
Cover by Brett Neiman

ISBN: 978-0-9836073-0-4

Contents

Prologue vii
Author's Note xi
Sweet as Lab 1
Lovely Hands 3
New Guy in Town 5
Blood 9
Beyond 13
Mr. Chin 17
Pet Dog 21
Power 27
Nice Legs 31
BaaaBurgers 35
Tied Up 39
The Howling 43
Isolation 45
Swine Dreamin' 47
Happy Barf 53

Time to Think	57
What the Hell Is That?	61
The Cat	65
You Can't Have My Liver, Mate	67
Problems, I Have Problems	71
Return of the Steak	73
Country Boys	77
Dad	81
Hangaroa Trip	85
Exorcism	89
Everything Is Better with Gravy	93
Shocked	97
Getting Soft	99
Grooving	103
Beach Night	105
The Kill	111
Short but Fun	115
Good Morning	117
Fishing with Tim	121
Everybody on the Bed	125
Connection	127
Meat Bananas	133
Coming to America!	137
A Note from Ryan	143
Acknowledgments	145
About Ryan Chin	147

Prologue

I follow Dad down the stairs and build speed across the lawn. He opens the truck's door, and I eye the opening, calculate my trajectory, and leave the ground. Even with the running start, my rear lags, the thousands of previous leaps and bounds taking their toll. On cue, Dad is there with a perfectly timed shove on my furry ass, and I'm into my copilot seat ready for another fishing trip. Surrounded by a cloud of cream fur, I hack like an old man needing another puff from his inhaler, and rest my chin on the hair-caked armrest.

It's embarrassing needing that nudge into the truck, but my snout is white, and that damn mole on my cheek grows bigger every day. Some would say these are my golden years, but that's bullshit because all my years are golden.

In my first golden year, I ate wild goat, buckets of lamb hearts, and beef livers. I didn't visit dog parks or go for leashed runs. I charged in one direction for miles—curling over horizons, stopping to lick my goods, and having deep thoughts on where I should piss. I figured I'd score with the local ladies and mark the same fence posts all my life—and I probably would have if I hadn't met Dad.

Actually, I take that back. I'd be decaying bone fragments if I hadn't met him, because I had a problem that first year. I chased sheep with intent to kill. In New Zealand, the place of my first golden year, chasing sheep is a capital crime punishable by gunshot. Finding Dad saved me and gave me the chance to run on both sides of the equator.

I've killed sheep in New Zealand, pinned down calves in California, and terrorized elk in Oregon. Dad and I have forded rivers in New Zealand, California, Oregon, Washington, and Canada. We're into our twelfth year together now—all golden.

I've led him through marriage, the funny thing humans do where they agree on nothing but still create beauty. And in the past six years, I've nuzzled and guided him through the challenges of fatherhood. He has his ups and downs like everyone else; however, I think it's a bit

Prologue

more with him being a writer. Putting yourself out there in any form of creative expression isn't easy.

Many hours have been spent listening to the sound of Dad's fingers on a keyboard, his toes massaging the muscles between my shoulder blades. All that tapping and the smile on his face at his book launch made me think it might be fun to stop lounging around as a foot warmer and share my story, tell it from Big Head's point of view.

So as we New Zealanders like to say, I'm giving it a go, mate!

My name is Big Head, I'm a yellow Lab, and this is my story.

I picked this picture because I look old and wise
— you know, like a writer…

Author's Note

I know what you're thinking: How can a dog read, write, and speak with such eloquence? I wish it was as easy as saying I mutated after a lightning strike or that I accidentally wandered onto a nuclear testing site. It'd be simple if I could just reminisce about the day I ate alphabet soup like Martha the talking dog, but in my case there are no answers—there's just a good story.

You hear accounts of children born with detailed memories from a past life. Maybe I'm one of those stories. Perhaps my heightened conscience is like how select humans can recite infinite numbers of pi for hours, and how certain humans learn new languages in a day, and how toddlers can pick up a musical instrument and jam with

The Big Head Diaries

no prior experience. I'm not touting myself as a genius; it's just—not all Labs are created equal.

I understand that humans question everything. That giant frontal lobe is prone to doubt. Doubt in others and—most damaging—doubt in yourselves. Part of our jobs as dogs is to help you believe, to inspire a run to the horizon without looking back. And we are here to lighten shit up.

Give yourself a break from worrying about your job, money, and when you are going to return that thing you didn't need to buy in the first place. Stop reading about world hunger, the refugee crisis, global warming, deforestation, *Fifty Shades of Grey*, and species on the edge of extinction.

And damn.

Stop questioning how a yellow Lab named Big Head knows so much.

Sweet as Lab

NEW ZEALAND

My eyes peel open for the first time. I see light and blurry movement but can't quite make out the nipple I've suckled for days. Whimpers surround me. I paw my way to a new position and latch on. My brothers and sisters ram their snouts at me, but I don't budge. Many dogs would say the milk is sweet, but since I'm in New Zealand, the milk isn't just sweet—it's *sweet as, mate*! Whimpers stop. I can hear Mother's heartbeat.

Our stomachs full, my siblings and I burrow into each other until we lose track of whose rear is whose—a maelstrom of yellow Lab. We snore away, and our drool becomes one.

Lovely Hands

My bro grinds into me. I stay latched to the prime nipple. I sprawl. My wide base holds me in position despite his efforts. My focus is sharp now; my brothers and sisters look like me: floppy ears, a snout, and black eyes. Our legs no longer shake and tremble with each step. The constant jockeying and Mom's milk have made us strong.

The Big Head Diaries

A door opens, and Mom darts outside, abruptly ending our meal. We whimper as humans approach. Mom's milk is forgotten as hands cup me, rub me, and stroke me. The hands send my tail into uncontrollable circles.

I look up into the eyes of a lady with a round face. Her lips curl up at the edges, and her eyes gleam. My tail whips faster. She reaches down and cups my head with one hand then runs her other hand down my back, engulfing my body in bliss. The pressure on my cheekbones and spine sends me into uncontrollable whimpers, different than the ones I made snuggled up to Mom. After a few minutes of this, she scoops those lovely hands under me.

As I'm carried off, I watch my brothers and sisters jockey for position waiting for Mom to return. Without me, there will be more milk for them.

The woman hops into a truck and places me in a box at her feet. She continues to rub me with those beautiful hands. As we bounce along, I hear her talk to the driver.

"Big Head. His name will be Big Head."

The driver responds, "Hah! Sweet as. After your old man, eh?"

New Guy in Town

I slide around in the cardboard box. New smells rush in through the open window. I can see up the lady's nose and blue sky out the window as we whizz along. I rear up; my paws barely catch the top of the box.

The lady reaches down for me and says, "You want to see what's up, eh, Big Head?"

After she rests me on her lap, I curl my front paws on the window's edge with my back paws on the lady's thigh. We slow down and enter an area with boarded-up buildings and a spattering of houses. Near an outhouse, railroad tracks shiny enough to be active extend into the distance. Kids streak by and run alongside our car. The lady waves at them as we pull up to a house. She opens the truck door.

The Big Head Diaries

As soon as my feet hit the ground, dogs and puppies rush to check me out, the new guy in town. The locals need to smell my goods, size me up. One dude nudges me too hard, so I muster my three-month-old growl. He backs off as I saunter over to a fence post. I lift my leg and spray as high as I can; height matters, as it shows how big I am. Satisfied that I'm cool, the dogs disperse. I lower my leg and take in my surroundings.

Young men in black leather jackets mingle about drinking from red-tinted bottles. One of them tosses an empty bottle toward a ditch. It shatters, and the rest of the men laugh. I think it's lame because that glass can cut my paws.

One man turns to another and they high-five. "Sweet, bro!"

Even though it's hot, the men don black leather jackets with the words *Black Power* written across the front and back. Many of the jackets have a giant clenched fist patched on the back. When men clench their fists, it's like a dog baring his teeth. Today though, everyone is chilling.

I turn my attention away from the men and run to the end of the driveway. A pack of children, some on foot and some on bicycles, meander up the street. More children play on a hillside near a group of buildings. I hear someone call it a school.

There's the sound of a motorbike in the distance. Sweeping hills surround me, and I know there's a river

New Guy in Town

nearby named Mohaka because I heard people talk about how fish called *kahawai* are packed in the river right now. In a paddock, yapping dogs crowd sheep into a tight circle.

I take a few steps toward the sheep and lift my nose. This is the loveliness I've smelled since I was born! Sticking my head through the barbed-wire fence, I notice a man has a sheep hanging in a shed. He's yanking on the skin, exposing the luscious red meat. The breeze delivers wafts of bloody tang. These are not just smells; this is an aroma. The sight of the sinuous lines of muscle along the sheep's back makes me pant. My eyes are fixed; drool floods my mouth.

The man flicks his knife at the ground. Even at this distance, I see the tantalizing drops of blood elongate before they splat onto the dirt. Other dogs circle and lick at the blood splatters, waiting for a scrap. I head around the barbed-wire paddock to get my fill, but then I hear the lady who brought me here.

"Big Head! Big Head! Come here, boyee!" she yells. She kneels down and slaps at her thighs as she repeats my name over and over. I think of those lovely hands again and rush up to her.

Blood

My eyes open. I stretch and look from the deck of the house. While many of the other dogs bed down in kennels, it appears I'm allowed to sleep anywhere. Last night the lady led me to this area and gave me a good rubdown.

"Sleep under the veranda, Big Head. I'll see you in the morning," she said as she walked away.

From the veranda I scan buildings on a hilltop. I heard people call it a school and say that the kids would return soon. The sun hits the rooftops, but down here the dew is heavy and chill is still in the air. I walk over to a fence pole, lift my leg, and wonder if I should paw at the front door because I'm hungry.

The Big Head Diaries

The sound of a motorbike catches my attention, and I eye it as it closes in on the yard. The herding dogs follow in tight formation. A big man with a moustache sways in the seat with each bump and dip. A skinned wild goat is strapped to the back of the motorbike, its limp head and legs bouncing.

As we Kiwis say, "That's the one, mate!"

Drool fills my mouth. The pig-hunting dogs sniff the air, circle in their cages, and lick their lips. In New Zealand, people in the countryside have herding dogs, pig-hunting dogs, and pet dogs. Feeding all of us could potentially empty one's wallet, but luckily there's fresh food running in these hills. The man stops; the herding dogs pull at the carcass, but the straps hold tight. The pig-hunting dogs headbutt the kennel doors.

The man shoos the herding dogs out of the way and unstraps the goat. With a heave and a thud, breakfast is served. I barge in, hoping for a bloody chunk before the big boys arrive. I bite down and hear the kennel gates open behind me. A Rottweiler bulls me out of the way and nips a few of the dogs that are too close for his liking.

The pig-hunting dogs take top dog honors around here by sheer size. Several of them have scars from their battles with wild boars. Pig hunters usually have a mix: smaller and faster dogs to run and corner the pig until the bruiser dogs like the Rotts arrive to hold the pig. Once the pig is secure, the hunter jumps in with a knife and

Blood

slits the pig's throat. Some dudes shoot the pig, but the cool guys use a blade.

Maybe one day I'll be a holding dog. Maybe one day I'll have a cool master who stabs pigs and boasts about Big Head the great pig hunter. For now though, fresh goat is the only thing on my mind. I circle in search of an opening and sneak in near the goat's rear. It's not a prime position, but unlike humans, I'm grateful for what I have. Ass meat never tasted so good.

Beyond

My feet still feel too big for my body. Humans might describe it as trying to run in oversized socks, but what do humans know? Humans buy special shoes for running, and they have races where they run in circles. I've also heard they run in place on machines that cost thousands of dollars.

Running is as simple as looking to the horizon and going hard. Today I'm bolting with my mate Memphis.

The Big Head Diaries

He's a Jack Russell. For a little twerp, he sure can move. I give chase and he cuts back and forth, but I stay the course and run right through him. Like an open-side flanker in rugby, I'm a punisher.

Looking over my shoulder, I see him tumble. We're young; we're durable. Flipping head over heels for ten meters is all in a day's fun. He's back up in a flash and angles toward me. Maybe if he played rugby, one of New Zealand's religions, he'd know how to take me down using technique instead of brute force, like I do. Instead of barreling into me, though, he falls into line behind me. A wise choice.

Here on the east coast of New Zealand's North Island, visible horizons extend in every direction. Native bush used to cover the lands on which I now run, but it was burned long ago to make way for grass. Sheep—those tasty buggers—need a lot of grass to eat. Patches of native bush still thrive in the gullies and along the river nearby. I'll explore the bush one day because deer live in there.

Memphis breaks out of my draft and accelerates past me. I kick it up another notch. We follow the contours of the land, paws barely touching the ground, riding a blanket of speed and joy. Like a pair of fighter jets in formation, we disappear over a hill that minutes ago was our horizon. We've never gone this direction, and my neck cranes at the vastness. At my young age, I've learned this is one of the greatest pleasures in life: going beyond where one can see—only to find more to explore.

Beyond

It's that time of day when our fur shines and breaths deepen. Fern trees peek over the canyon's edge sporting their vibrant greens as they sway and bow in the evening winds. Panting, we stop and lap at our goods. Our gaze shifts behind us then back to the uncharted horizons. The hills invite us to continue, but our long shadows point us home. I give Memphis a lick, and we trot off.

With the last rays of the sun piercing long wisps of clouds, I understand why locals refer to New Zealand as Aotearoa, land of the long white cloud. Now there is no chasing, no barking—just two mates side by side in stride. The sun dips, golds turn to crimsons, and I can't help feeling sorry for humans running in circles.

Mr. Chin

I charge up the hill with Memphis on my heels. Moments ago we frolicked and pawed at each other, lost in puppy play, but now we move with purpose, our heads down and our gaits in sync. The kids are back in school, and with kids there is dropped food. Nothing will go to waste.

We reach the school and circle around to the playground. The little kids congregate on the play structure while the big kids juggle a soccer ball between scattered cow patties. Not once do they allow the ball to bounce in the fresh mess. This is a school where you learn things, and I reckon learning to deal with shit is as good a lesson as any.

The girls whip crisp passes to each other and shoot hoops on a basketball court, no doubt practicing for their upcoming netball season. Netball is similar to basketball with the hoop, but it also has major differences. Dribbling is not allowed, and there is no backboard attached to the hoop.

I scurry out of the way of the ball and lap up a potato chip. Memphis splits off; our friendship doesn't involve sharing food. It's a little early for lunchtime, but there's still bounty to hunt. A chip here, a cracker there, and a moldy sandwich discarded into the bushes. The chip is still crunchy—freshly dropped—so I perk up my ears and scan the yard, listening for the telltale crinkle of a chip bag. I hone in on a girl with her back toward me. She tosses a bag in the rubbish bin and brushes her hands on her pants. Too late! Another target, however, is sitting under an awning and opening his lunch box.

I've learned that if I wrinkle my forehead and cock my head just right, food will come my way. If I run into a tough customer, then I give them the Lab eyes. Humans succumb to these big black puppy eyes.

You will give me food. You will give me food now.

As I make my way across the paved area, a girl yells, "It's Big Head!"

The kids swarm like ants on honey. I flip onto my back to expose my belly. Through the maelstrom of petting and patting and through the legs of a little girl, I see a man

Mr. Chin

standing behind them. If he had a tail, it'd be between his legs.

In addition to smelling goats miles away and sensing buckets of beef livers through closed doors, I know when humans need me to drool on their legs. It's a proven fact that dog drool lowers blood pressure, reduces the risk of heart attack, and increases smiling. That guy needs a slobbering in a big way. His short hair is black like most of the people around here, but his skin is lighter, his nose is flatter, and his eyes are skinnier.

Before I can reach him, though, Principal Angie comes out and yells, "No animals on the school grounds!"

Suddenly, the petting turns to slapping. One boy even gives me a light boot to the rear. How quickly the energy changes from glee to aggression—time to evacuate! Over my shoulder I see the man wipe his eyes with his sleeves and can still feel his gaze on me as Memphis and I duck under a fence.

As we slow our run, I can still hear the conversation.

"You didn't have to kick him," says the man.

"We had to get him out of here, Mr. Chin! Miss said so."

Memphis and I stop at the edge of the Mohaka River to stare out at the wide valley. Goats graze on the opposite bank. As we dive into the canyon, I can't get the man's sad face out of my Big Head. Ferns and branches whip by, and I decide right then that I can help Mr. Chin feel better. I'll find him tomorrow.

Pet Dog

The veranda turns out to be a nice place to bed down. Even though I'm not allowed inside, sometimes they leave the door open and I can see and hear the TV. I don't mean to watch, but at night it's on for hours. I see the back of a man's head and his feet propped up. He's constantly changing the channels. Through the rapid fire of images and audio, I end up learning a lot about humans.

One show has a tall, gray-haired man with glasses. He must enjoy making people fight, because after he talks, people scream at each other, swing punches, and occasionally throw chairs. Men rush to stop the fighting, and after everyone settles down, people chant his name.

Jerry! Jerry! Jerry!

I can't throw chairs, but I can relate to swinging punches. The alpha dogs around here try to bully me, but with my Big Head comes a big attitude. Maybe one day Jerry will have us on his show.

The boy who lives here likes watching fights where men bash each other and never seem to get hurt. When a man flies through the air off the top rope, you'd think the guy on the bottom would get crushed, but he usually bounces up, kicks ass, and ends up winning. Weird.

Then there's the shooting, car chases, hiding, screaming, and running. It appears humans fight a lot.

My favorite part of TV though is the food. Sizzling meats, oozing sauces, and people stuffing their faces with french fries make for good dreams. I'm not so certain about the images of dogs running to eat what looks like bowls of goat shit, though. Must be fake.

The TV occupies me, but it's the clatter of cheerful humans through the open door that comforts me. This family laughs a lot. The lady who took me here is the mom of the house. Her smile and laugh match her booming voice. The kids are lucky to have her and an equally kind father in their lives. Many of the children

Pet Dog

around here are not as fortunate. Without loving parents in their lives, many of the local boys appear to have a permanent growl.

There's one kid whom I try to cheer up, but it's like there's a wall around him. His shoulders slump, his head hangs, and when he talks, it's in short, aggressive bursts. I leap, I bound, I run circles around him trying to get him to chase me. If he would just kneel, I'd give him a big lapping kiss. At my young age, I understand part of my job is to help humans smile. Happy dogs create happy people and vice versa.

Speaking of making people stoked, I won't say I've changed Mr. Chin, but he can't help but give me a pat on the head and a belly rub when I stroll through the school grounds. He doesn't have to wipe his eyes when he sees me anymore; I'm damn good at my job.

I know where he lives but haven't visited him at home yet since the school is on the way to my charging grounds. It's convenient to pop in for attention from Mr. Chin before I laser to the horizon with my pack.

Besides Memphis, I have other mates now. There's a shepherd mix retired from herding. His once sleek coat is matted and large patches of his fur are missing. He limps when he walks and sways from the slightest breeze when he's standing, but when we run, we are equals. His spirit charges and his body follows. He seems to know each bound and each drop of drool sheared into the wind may

The Big Head Diaries

be his last. There's another Jack Russell who may or may not be related to Memphis, a massive pit bull mix capable of biting my big head off in a single chomp, and a half dozen other random dogs that come and go.

After slipping through a barbed-wire fence, we usually bolt for a few minutes then stop at the crest of a hill to work out our pecking order. We wrestle, roll, growl, and snarl for long minutes before we're off and running again. I'm not top dog around here, but no one gives me any shit either. I'm cool with that. The impromptu battles with my furry mates are fun but far from comforting. It doesn't send my tail into uncontrollable circles.

Besides Mr. Chin, no one pays much attention to me now. My puppy fur has given way to a coarser coat, and instead of that new-to-the-world fragrance, I reek of sheep shit with hints of my latest bloody meal.

Each day, I feel faster, more powerful. All this is good, but I miss the human hands. Every day the herding dogs head out with their masters. When I try tagging along, their master yells, "Git!"

Last weekend when the pig dogs were loaded up for a hunt, I leaped into the back and was yanked out. They took off, leaving me behind in a swirl of dust.

In a way I have it better than the pig dogs and the herding dogs, since they sleep in kennels at night. Sometimes I feel they are jealous of my spot on the veranda and my freedom. But what is freedom without purpose?

Pet Dog

I know I'm a pet dog, but aren't pet dogs supposed to receive attention?

I want a Master; I need a Master.

Power

The kids from the preschool cry as they parade up the driveway where Mr. Chin waits. He leads them into the main building, where the older children are gathered, comforting them with a gentle squeeze on the shoulder as they enter. The kids sense the urgency; their tiny hearts thump and race.

Remember that clenched-fist symbol decorating the clothing worn by the men around here? I've learned that is the logo for the Black Power, one of the two major Maori gangs in New Zealand. The other major Maori gang is the

The Big Head Diaries

Mongrel Mob, and the two of them have been growling at each other for decades.

Everyone is too occupied to notice me on the school grounds, so I set myself up in the shade near the main entrance to keep up on the drama. Unbelievably, right in front of me there happens to be residue left over from a type of meat. It could be pureed liver, or maybe it's vomit. It's dried and crusty, but with enough licking it turns into a perfectly aged pâté. Lovely.

The mystery blob turns out to be the quite the snack. As I lap away, I get the feeling that if humans had hair on their backs, it'd be standing. Adults are coming and going with their hands on their hips, and short bursts of chatter fill the air. The school secretary's eyes bug out as she makes phone call after phone call.

Angie pulls Mr. Chin aside. "Here's the story. Mob members tried to rob a Black Power member's home. The Black Power man came home and shot at them. Looks like at least one Mob member is dead, and there's heavy talk about retaliation. Mob members may be on their way here right now."

Apparently, our little town is a Black Power stronghold sandwiched between towns to the north and south that are ruled by the Mongrel Mob. More information trickles in. Police formed a roadblock to stop any Mob members out for revenge. I process all this as I finish my pâté, and I get it. It's like two packs of wild dogs who don't like each other. But instead of marking territory by pissing high on fences or trees, these humans use guns to spray bullets at each other's houses when they are mad.

Humans leave me in awe at times—their unwillingness to forgive and their habit of making the same mistakes over and over. You'd think that after decades of disagreement, shootings, and killings they would have worked something out by now. I know dogs scrap all the time, but at least after we fight we lick each other's penises and run to the horizon together like nothing ever happened.

Nice Legs

I'm tucked under a hedge at the edge of the schoolyard, watching the kids and gnawing a cow leg that I found. I think someone may have helped themselves to a cow, because I found it in a secluded area outside a paddock. Around here if someone's cow wanders onto your property, then it's fair game. Poaching is also a legal activity in this region. Whenever I clamp down on an animal part, I can't help but sing.

> *I see skies of blue and clouds of white*
> *Animal parts for me to bite*
> *And I think to myself, what a wonderful world.*

The Big Head Diaries

Mr. Chin carves around on a skateboard, showing the boys how it's done. Angie told him he has to watch being too friendly with the boys or he may risk losing their respect. Personally, I think he gains their respect by interacting with them. Us dogs look up to leaders of the pack, and so do humans.

A lot of the boys around could use a dude in their lives like Mr. Chin. It's funny. One moment the boys love him, and the next moment they are swearing at him and giving him shit. He finds a balance between being a hard-ass and showing massive care that many of them have never experienced. Of course he can't replace a missing dad, but maybe he'll influence them enough to stay out of trouble. Most of the boys have goals of one day being in the Black Power as a fully patched member, a fine goal I reckon as long as it's not their only goal.

On one paw, I believe the gang stuff is cool. It provides community, brotherhood, and a sense of security.

On the other paw, I think it can be too extreme, too fundamental. Mr. Chin's neighbor was recently shot while he was eatin' fish-and-chips in a parked car. The guy who shot him isn't tough. He's a coward.

I'm through the bone now and into fresh marrow. I concentrate on extracting the succulence, but my tongue is too short and stout. It's not shaped to extract sweetness like a hummingbird's tongue; the broad surface is made for sloppy kisses. I grind on the edges and adjust

Nice Legs

my angles until a big hunk of bone cracks away with the marrow still attached. It's like the perfect mouthful of chocolate and peanut butter or a well-balanced spoonful of potatoes and gravy.

The sun sweeps, clouds roll, and I grind away. Down to hoof now and satisfied. I bury the other leg and head out in search of Memphis.

BaaaBurgers

Bugger, mate! Some mutt took the other cow leg I stashed, and this morning I was booted by the big dogs from the goat carcass. By the time they left, there were just a few bone fragments. I can't help myself. There is food everywhere. I just need to catch and kill it myself.

I spot goats in the distance, and I close in. Several large billies with horns mingle with the nannies and kids. I'm not sure about tangling with a big billy on my own, but hunger drives me toward them. They lift their heads in unison and trot away. While the kids and nannies have a sense of urgency about them, the billies look as though they are peeling themselves from a dinner table and are ready for a nap. A big surly one takes a few bites of grass as he rambles down a narrow path and stops to look over his shoulder.

"What are you going to do now?" he seems to say.

I know when I'm beat.

I understand chasing sheep may get me killed, but it's impossible to get away from them, and they smell so good! I heard someone inform Mr. Chin that sheep outnumber people in New Zealand. People make carpet, socks, and clothes out of the sheep. I don't need a sweater. I need lunch.

My stomach churns. A dog must do what he has to do to survive, so I bolt to the nearest paddock in search of an easier meal. I eye the barbed-wire fence. Slipping under the bottom wire is safer, but that means losing my speed. Without breaking stride I leap between the strands of wires, extending my legs at just the right moment with the perfect trajectory, risking that which I enjoy licking. Snagging my goods is not an option.

Once I'm in the paddock, the sheep turn their heads and run. They sense I am not a herding dog and know I am out for blood.

I zero in on a lamb. The herd scatters, and I have trouble staying on target. I'm like a crazed man at an all-you-can-eat buffet. My plate will be piled high. I hear barking and yelling, and soon the herding dogs are on me, snarling and guiding me away from those they are sworn to protect.

I try to state my case, remind them of who they are and what they eat.

"Mate. It's food! Tasty lamb chops. Lamb hearts!"

I try bribery.

"Mate. Let me kill one, and I'll drop off a shoulder and a fat leg!"

Then blackmail.

"I know where your family lives!"

It's no use. They are too brainwashed by the Man.

I veer off and never look back. A hunter is not always successful. Next time I will make the kill.

Tied Up

It's no use. Teeth are no match for metal; this time they put a chain on me. I thought tying me to a tree with a rope was meant to be a challenge. In the past few weeks, I've made quick work of little ropes, big ropes, and doubled-up ropes. Sometimes they wouldn't even bother to cut away the old ropes, which has resulted in a nice collection around my neck. I didn't mind, but it irked Mr. Chin, because he cut away my rope trophies.

I learned Mr. Chin is from America, and he came here to teach after his dog died. That's why his imaginary tail was between his legs when he first saw me. Seems like he's healing though, as he gave it to me good when I ran up to him. He rubbed my head, grabbed a cheek and a

The Big Head Diaries

paw, and flipped me over. My soft underfur filled the air when he raked my belly, and whimpers spilled out of me uncontrollably. Memphis says Mr. Chin's belly rubs are mean as!

If you haven't picked up on how New Zealanders use the word *as*, allow me to explain. Just think of it as a create-your-own metaphor. Things can be sweet as, mean as, and even sad as. Try it. You'll think it's cool as.

I was tuned in to the sound of Mr. Chin's old red van, and I would run after it when he chugged up the hill to the school. If I timed it right, I'd be right there as he pulled up, with full-on tornado tail. Sometimes he'd burst out the door and sprint up to the rugby field, spinning and yelling, "C'mon, Big Head!" Then with both of us panting, he'd wrestle me to the ground. Afterward I'd follow him to his classroom and hang out by the door.

Once the school bell rang, though, I knew to leave. It was total bullshit that I, a relatively clean dog, could not be on the school grounds when escaped cows and sheep routinely crapped on the schoolyard and families of filthy pigs rooted around the play structure.

Angie, the principal, enforced the rule of no animals on the school grounds. So after the brief morning visits, I'd wait until the kids left for more of Mr. Chin's rubdowns.

It was a sweet-as routine: chewing through my rope in the morning, hunting for food, and then finding

Tied Up

Mr. Chin after school. None of that matters anymore, though, as my life is now a six-foot-diameter area around a tree.

This chain has ruined everything.

The Howling

I tear at the old meat and drag the chain over to my water dish. People stack firewood in neat piles, smoke hangs heavy in the evenings, and yellow leaves blow from the trees. The attitudes have been chill like the weather. No gang violence to speak of since the last episode.

From my chain I can hear the kids up at the school, and sometimes I can even hear Mr. Chin's voice. His voice is deep and comforting—full of love—even when he raises his voice with the children. He's not exactly yelling at the children; he just wants them to live up to their potential. Many of the boys are almost as big as him, their voices changing and hormones raging—ready to bring it. I wonder what Mr. Chin would do if someone picked a fight with him. Would he bring it?

He passes by daily, his van grinding along in first gear. I wonder if he knows I'm here and wonder if he misses giving me belly rubs. I heard him talk about his old dog. It was a chow–golden retriever mix that only lived six years. Six years isn't long, but if his dog hadn't died, then Mr. Chin wouldn't be here bonding with a class of Maori children. Everything happens for a reason. I once heard Mr. Chin chuckling about the gang madness with a local, and also commenting on how blessed he feels experiencing intimate moments with the community.

Recently, there was a Maori funeral called a *tangi* for a village elder. As the casket was brought out, the men and women broke into a *haka* to protect her and send her off. The haka is a traditional Maori song and dance with many forms, each one for different situations, each one chilling. Even I feel the power.

During the tangi, I received a lot of delicious food scraps, but mostly people just ignored me. Even Mr. Chin mingled with the locals. He only gave me a quick head-pat and moved on.

I can bark, I can whimper, and I can growl. Today I'm so hungry and cold and want so badly to feel human hands on me that I howl for the first time. Humans might even call it crying.

Awrrrrooooooooooooooooooooo! Whoooorrrrrrooooo.

Isolation

Bare tree branches click in the wind, and smoke rises from chimneys, a gray snake dissipating into the skies. My breath is slow like my thoughts. I exhale. Vapor clouds my vision, blurs my misery. Frost covers the ground except for the small area around my snout. If someone moved me, there'd be an imprint of my body. All night I allowed the leaves to pile against me for warmth. The leaves gave me insulation from the cold ground but not much.

The skies are clear, and the sun shows on the hilltops. Though some may see the frost melting at first light as beautiful, I see it as the end of a long, cold night and the beginning of another lonely day. Even Memphis stopped visiting me. Frost melts and warmth at last.

The Big Head Diaries

But what's this? No more chain? Downward dog and upward dog to loosen the muscles and a head shake to rid myself of the chain's imprint. Sheep in a nearby paddock munch away, oblivious to my freedom. I trot toward them but catch sight of a fresh goat carcass near the herding dogs' kennels. I slink over and look around, waiting to be yelled at. No one around, so I bury my face in the goodness.

Off in the distance I hear men chatting and see them in a nearby shed hoisting a freshly killed pig by its hind legs. Once it's secure they pull at the skin. That sound, like fabric ripping, means a waft of pork chops will soon fill the air. A shiver of joy runs through me. This must be how kids feel unwrapping candy. The men notice me and wave me over.

"Big Head! Some pig for ya, boy?" they ask.

I take off running. Maybe they will give me a belly rub too!

Then the chain pulls tight, and I'm back to the cold, the hunger, the isolation.

How long have I been here?

How long will this go on?

Awrrrroooooooooooooooooooooo! Whoooorrrrrrooooo!

Swine Dreamin'

I leap into the back of the truck with a half dozen dogs and shuffle into a tight corner. The truck lurches away, and I stay steady as the other dogs give me the once-over. I'm like the new kid who saunters onto the schoolyard and picks up a ball. How far and how fast can I throw? Will I hesitate at crunch time, or will I nail the game winner?

I must perform, not be a detriment to the hunt. I must run faster than ever and be ready to sacrifice my body for a kill. No one will tell me to stop as I clamp down on a bloody throat. Copying the other dogs, I sit on my haunches and stare back at our dust trail; we are soldiers ready for the drop zone. This would be a perfect opportunity to light a cigarette and pretend to chill—if

The Big Head Diaries

I smoked. Besides the rumble of the tires on gravel, the wind, and the pounding of our hearts, the troops are silent. The threat of death is real for dogs on a pig hunt.

A heavy Rott and a mastiff sway with each bounce and turn; their stout bodies and scarred faces give them a stoic look. Four smaller dogs sit ready to explode out of the gate. They are the chasers; they will take point in the hunt and corner the pig. Speed, endurance, and iron nerves are needed. We are not hunting cuddly piglets or peaceful pigs like the ones that root around the school's playground. We are hunting feral hogs weighing up to four hundred pounds. Their razor-sharp tusks can be as long as my head—enough to gore and kill a dog or a human.

In addition to Australian possums, rats, and feral cats, wild pigs are another invasive mammal in New Zealand that tilts the ecosystem out of balance. Introduced by explorers and settlers, they quickly populated the countryside, rooted up native plants, and decimated the nests of native ground birds, including the kiwi, New Zealand's national icon. The hunting of pigs is a sport and a necessity for population control. There is no closed season or limit on wild pigs, and even if there was, I live in an area where everything is legal unless you get caught.

As we ramble deeper into the endless hills, I stare out at the horizons and let out a heavy sigh. This place—my home—is as beautiful as it gets. In my short life, I've come to love sprinting over the green waves to the horizon.

Swine Dreamin'

Another truck follows behind us pulling an ATV. Depending on the terrain we choose to hunt, the ATV comes in handy for packing out the bacon and chops. We charge down a gravel road for many dusty miles before we ascend a steep grade. The drivers open and close stock gates as we pick our way across open range. The day is overcast and humid, rain imminent.

We stop at the edge of a deep valley. River sounds ride the heavy air up the valley sides and fade into the gray skies above. A tall, lanky man with a large knife hanging from his belt opens the tailgate, and we spill out. The other dogs bark with excitement, and I join in.

The hunters discuss strategy and kneel in an area where pigs rooted up the ground. One man rolls the soil in his hands to read the signs. Puffs of smoke hang over his shoulder: How many pigs, how big, and where did they go from here?

The men decide to follow the rim of the valley to a deep gully where native bush still thrives. It's easy to see how the native bush survived the clearing fires in the gullies protected by the topography of the land. As we reach the junction where the gully feeds into the larger river valley, one of the men waves his arms and whistles. The dogs yap to pump each other up then disappear into the dense vegetation.

The Rott and mastiff follow along, unconcerned that they cannot keep up with the smaller dogs. I'm an in-between size: too large and muscular for the long distance and speed needed for tracking down a pig and not as burly as the Rott for holding the pigs. What I do have, though, is a determination to prove myself, and sometimes that trumps physical attributes. I'll do what I can. Within minutes, the dogs yap and bark, and the Rott picks up the pace.

One man, who moments ago slogged along with a cigarette in the corner of his mouth, jolts into a sprint. Clouds of smoke puff over his head as his strides lengthen. He yells over his shoulder, "That's the one, mate!"

I dive in behind them, ferns whipping my face. My speed overshoots my ability to react, but I trust those ahead of me. I follow their path and lean into blind corners at full stride. My paws leave the ground as I leap moss-covered logs without knowing what's on the other side.

The dogs' ruckus grows louder. They are no longer moving away from us; a pig or pigs must be cornered. My heart races as my paws and body float over the forest floor. I burst into a clearing and see a giant boar with tusks to match. The Rott already has a hold of its rear leg. The boar turns and catches the Rott with a slicing upward movement. The scarred-face warrior yelps; the men shout.

The Rott bleeds on the ground; a gurgle rattles from his throat. On cue the mastiff steps in and latches onto the same leg. I dart in at the same time. The boar sees my

Swine Dreamin'

movement and turns, but I juke my body, barely slipping past the menacing tusks, and clamp onto the leg opposite of the mastiff. The hunter with the large knife moves in, and I pull with all my might to spread the legs and render the boar immobile. The knife finds its mark, and after a piercing squeal, there is calm.

I feel scruff hands on my head telling me to let go. My tail windmills in large circles as the men pat me and discuss how Big Head saved the day.

My body goes cold like the pig, and I am awake. The chain is still there, the grass stiff with frost. I lick my lips. What an incredible dream. I was receiving the thing I seek the most—attention and praise. The fresh bacon was going to be sweet as, too.

Happy Barf

Mr. Chin's van pulls up to the house. My muscles explode to attention, pulling the chain to its limits. My tail windmills like never before. It's a good thing nothing nearby is fragile; whirling Lab tails can be dangerous.

When Mr. Chin rounds the corner and heads toward me, I pull harder. Barking turns to whimpering.

He walks up matter-of-factly, unclips the chain, and says, "C'mon, boy. Let's go to the beach."

I know I could bolt, chase sheep, and run to the horizon by myself, but I'm curious about this place called the beach. Although I'm not religious, I believe thou shall not disobey the hand that frees you.

One question I do have for him, though, is, *What took you so long, mate?*

When dogs are sad, we howl, we yowl, we cry, and we whimper. Babies whimper and cry, but adults often forget to cry when they are sad. I heard Mr. Chin telling Angie that he cried every day for six months straight when his old dog died. The tears were also for a brother he lost.

I don't know what it feels like to lose someone I love, but witnessing the Maori funeral and being a part of Mr. Chin's healing, I know humans deal with death in different ways. Some cry, some get angry, and some may just hibernate and go silent. In Mr. Chin's case, after his dog died, he packed up his surfboards and fly rods and flew across the world to pursue his dreams of teaching overseas. And I'm glad he did, because now he is ready to hang!

He rips the sliding door open, and I jump into his red van, Lonna. It's been close to a year since I've ridden in a car, so I bound to the rear and back to the front. I thrust my nose out the window then dart to the rear again. Mr. Chin yells at me and slaps the passenger seat. When I

Happy Barf

sit in the seat, I'm inundated with the best rubs ever to grace my big head.

Maybe it's the sun on the western horizon or the long shadows in the river valley below, but everything feels slow. Road dust sucks through the loose-fitting doors and hangs in the air, pierced by the low-angle rays of light dancing through the windows. Lonna shakes and bounces. I'm so stoked I might throw up.

Mr. Chin notices the I'm-gonna-puke look and revs Lonna to her max. We skid to a halt just in time. He bursts out, runs around the front of the van, and yanks my door open. In an instant I'm on the beach for my first time.

Talk about horizons! Dark sand stretches as far as the eye can see in both directions. Sinuous lines of flotsam weave through the many logs deposited along the sands at high tide. Motion sickness subsided, I hit my stride, and my paw prints widen each second.

A smell, one I've never encountered, makes me curious. Sand flies as I dig in and change directions like a cop seeing his suspect and banging a U-turn. A fatty animal half buried in the sand is perfectly aged to my liking. I dig around, looking for a soft spot to tear into. I bury my snout and munch away, barely needing my teeth for the tender blubber. The texture, the aroma, and the oceanside seating take me away. All that's missing is a quartet and some Bach. The meat is so soft, I'm slurping more than biting. When I come up for a breath, I hear Mr. Chin.

He's just a dot in the distance, holding a log above his head and yelling. Stomach full, I turn and charge. As I approach, he sidesteps and swings the log into the swirling froth at the ocean's edge. No one has ever thrown anything for me, but I know what to do. A wave pushes the log in, and I leap over the incoming whitewash. My jaws clamp down on the log. I'm surprised at the satisfaction it gives me. Instead of returning it peacefully, I make Mr. Chin tug on the log, growling and tearing at the saturated wood. Again and again we do this, until there's a pile of rotten wood chips at the water's edge and we can hardly see. Who would have thought playing with something besides animal parts could be so fun?

On the way home, I barf decayed marine mammal all over the van, filling the passenger door storage pocket with the putrid mess—a token of my appreciation to Mr. Chin. Judging by his smile and laughter, I think he liked it.

He pulls up to my house, apologizes to me, and clips me back to the chain.

Time to Think

Buds poke through the branches of the tree I'm tied to. The towering firewood stacks have dwindled. Mr. Chin's students have grown an inch, and he has new entrants. In New Zealand kids can start school the day they turn five. A pair of twin girls and a spunky boy recently started school, which swells his class size to eleven students. Not much, but with the multiage classes, he still has his hands full.

The nights aren't as cold, but they are still lonely. I live for the sound of Mr. Chin's van crunching the gravel in the driveway and his voice. He misses some days, but we've been hitting the beach or the river with frequency for weeks now.

The Big Head Diaries

The smell of my puke in the side door is still there. I heard a local talking to Mr. Chin about puking and how everyone overdoes it at times and how sometimes one tries to have too much fun. I'm a fast learner. Next time I find decayed marine mammal, I'll just slurp up enough for a snack instead of eating bucketsful.

Or as Mr. Chin joked to the local, "Take a few shots but don't drink the bottle!"

After our sorties Mr. Chin drops me off. The clip of the chain doesn't gut me anymore with our consistent schedule. It'd be amazing if he kept me down at his house, but I understand. He doesn't want to overstep his bounds by keeping me. As an outsider he must be careful around here, show massive respect, tread lightly, and have a little swagger as well.

The gangs have been quiet, but that's sure to change with the warmer weather. The boys sporting their blue, the Black Power color, walk around with their pants defying gravity and flash the signs to each other. Unlike the older men in the Black Power, there's a certain copycat demeanor with the younger men and prospects inspired by movies they have seen. The baggy pants and the crotch grab are all part of the act. It's a classic old-school and new-school scene.

In a way Mr. Chin is the perfect person to teach here. He is seen as a neutral party with no possible affiliations with rival gang members. People are curious and maybe

Time to Think

a little unsure about him. The previous two teachers had been threatened by a student's parent. That provided the vacancy for Mr. Chin. The man was destined to rub my belly.

I heard Angie, the school principal, talk to a lady about how Mr. Chin ended up here. Something about his van breaking down near the school, his sending a coffee-stained resume, and his showing up to the job interview barefoot, wearing surf shorts. Classic stuff that might make for a good book one day.

The attention he gives me and the way he pats my head and scratches behind my ears has me thinking. When did dogs come to love the touch of a human so much? Why do I feel the need to lick a human's face? In many ways it would be easier to be a wild animal instead of longing for attention from humans. Maybe Mr. Chin is part dog, because the way he wrestles with me is spot-on. He goes low on all fours, buries his shoulder and head into me, and plays fair for a while before busting out the advantage of his hands. Once he grabs my front paws and wraps my body, I know it's all over. In an instant, I'm flipped over.

Last night when he dropped me off, he left a log from the beach. Chewing on it gives me something to do. My teeth marks are all over it. I can't see Mr. Chin's handprints, but I know they are there. I sigh, and drift off with a paw on the log.

What the Hell Is That?

Mr. Chin unclips the chain and walks me to the van as usual. We head toward the beach, but he passes the turnoff. I leap to the back and stare out the window at the gravel road shrinking in the distance. Just like that, I'm farther away from home than I've ever been.

I ram my snout out the crack in the window, take in the smells, and think about all the new things I will piss on. There will be fresh horizons, new logs to kill, and maybe there will be a few extra sheep around that no one will miss. Problems, I have problems. We've established that.

After a month of sorties with Mr. Chin, I'm experienced: No more motion sickness. No more puking. And definitely no more gorging on bloated marine mammal.

The Big Head Diaries

I'm a real copilot, digging my claws into the worn plaid seat and swaying with each turn as naturally as wind-blown grasses dancing on the hillsides.

It doesn't look like we'll stop anytime soon. Mr. Chin adjusts his headphones and turns up the volume on his CD player. Occasionally he leans over and rubs the back of my neck. When I lie down on the seat, he runs his hand the length of my back and stops to pat my rump. He seems to get as much pleasure out of it as me. I sigh and fall asleep with his hand resting on my head.

When the van slows, I pop up and see more lights than I've ever seen. This must be a city. I take a big whiff and process all the layers. Even through the car exhaust fumes, rubbish, and wood smoke, I can smell a hint of sheep. My stomach rumbles, and I lick my nose.

Mr. Chin pulls into a brightly lit parking lot. He grabs my cheek and tells me to be a good boy before he hops out and runs into a store. This is the first time I've been left alone in a vehicle, so I do what any dog would do. I bark and hunt for something to chew. Given its proximity, the armrest seems like a reasonable place to start.

When Mr. Chin returns, he yells at me to stop barking, looks at the armrest, snatches my snout, and forces my face at the chewed area.

"No!" he yells.

I wrinkle my forehead and drop my head. "What the hell else was I supposed to do while I waited?"

What the Hell Is That?

He softens his tone and says, "Got some food for ya, boy."

When we arrive at his mate's house, Mr. Chin opens a crinkly bag, rummages around for a bowl, and pours some crunchy pellets into it. I sniff the air. It sort of smells like food—I think. I think back to the dogs eating this stuff on TV and realize it wasn't fake.

The pellets are exactly the size and shape of goat shit. I apologize for my language, but after a year of scarfing goats and sheep, and gorging on buckets of organs in their original state, I have no choice but to turn my head at the bowl.

I sit back with my head cocked and my dark lab eyes questioning Mr. Chin. "What the fuck is that?"

He pushes it closer. I back away. He stirs it and pushes the bowl at me. I back away farther. Then he laughs and rubs my head. We jump back in the van to go buy some steak, extra bloody.

The Cat

After a glorious weekend, Mr. Chin leads me into his house, and I'm greeted with a hiss. Normally, I ignore cats. If I harass an animal, it's for food. Cats don't have enough meat to mess with. I can't ignore her challenge though, so I pull on the leash and growl at the gray fur ball. She backs up, swats at the air, and shows her teeth. Mr. Chin leads me around to a room with glass doors. He sets up a blanket under a table, gives me a bowl of water, and leaves me.

I nose up against the glass doors and watch Mr. Chin tear up paper to light a fire. The cat saunters up to the door, knowing we are separated by glass, and hisses just centimeters from my face. I set my head down out of her

The Big Head Diaries

view, prompting her to butt her head against the glass. I lift my head suddenly to mess with her. She backs up, baring her teeth, and I can't help but feel like I won this one, even though that rug by the fire looks cozy.

Mr. Chin eases the door open and squeezes in to keep the cat and me separated. He bends down, gives my head a few strokes, and says, "That's Baetis. You will have to be cool; otherwise, this won't work. No more chain, buddy. You can stay with me."

He disappears behind a counter. There's the sound of those damn pellets being poured into a bowl and water running. Two bowls are set in front of me. I take a few laps of water, but I'm still not touching those pellets. I'll give him the big lab eyes in the morning and hopefully get a steak instead. Mr. Chin kneels down, holds his head to mine, and leaves.

Light from the fire flickers through the glass doors separating Baetis and me. I have a real home. I know Mr. Chin isn't staying here forever. How long will this last? I don't know, but I don't want it to end.

You Can't Have My Liver, Mate

The dew cools my paws. After slaughtering a barnacle-covered log for hours yesterday, my pads are raw. Licking them last night helped a little, but Mr. Chin kept telling me to *Shhhhhhhh* because he was trying to sleep. A lapping Lab tongue in a quiet room sounds like a sonic boom. Not wanting to ruin my inside privileges, I stopped. I'm one of the few dogs around who are allowed inside the house. From chain to a padded carpet inside a house—rags to riches, baby—that's me.

We're at school early; we both have work to do. I mark the flax plants around the schoolyard with Big Head juice. Mr. Chin unlocks the doors then picks up rubbish, jackets, and shoes. Unfortunately, it looks like the teens were

The Big Head Diaries

drinking on the school grounds again. He will have to pick up broken glass as well. After living here for eight months, he knows the drill. Drunk teens challenging his authority, broken glass, school lockdowns because of possible gang retaliation, escaped cows, and runaway kids barely faze him. He has the Kiwi attitude down.

He knows, "She'll be right, mate!"

I watch him sweep the glass, and I wonder why people trash their own homes. The teens breaking the bottles probably went to this school. They are brothers, sisters, and cousins of the children who attend the school now. As I stated before, I love humans, but they make no sense at times.

As Mr. Chin dumps the glass in the garbage, I notice a parent walking onto the playground carrying a bucket in each hand. Even though the man has tree-trunk legs and is twice as wide as Mr. Chin, he sways and leans a bit from the weight of the buckets. Flies buzz over the open tops. Drool fills my mouth and oozes out of the corners as he stops to talk to Mr. Chin.

"Mr. Chin! Few livers for Big Head?"

"He'd love that. Twins are doing great. Such a joy to have them in class."

"Thanks. They're having fun at school."

"That's my goal for these little guys. They have to like learning."

"Sweet as, Mr. Chin!"

You Can't Have My Liver, Mate

"See ya around, and thanks for the livers."

I'm right at Mr. Chin's side, jamming my snout at the bucket. He smiles, sets the bucket down, and reaches for one. I give him *the look*, wrinkle my forehead, and droop my head. "Just one, mate!"

He tosses it into the grass. The slimy coating makes it slide an extra meter. This isn't my first liver; I know exactly what to do.

Like kids and their lollipops, dogs eat beef livers in different ways too. There are biters, nibblers, lickers, and combinations of the aforementioned. When it comes to livers, I like the lick and gobble. Licking it gives me just the taste of blood. It gets the drool flowing. It's like rolling fine bourbon on your tongue or swirling cabernet in the glass before you sip it, something I've seen Mr. Chin do as he sits by the fire. After the licking, I chomp the gelatinous wonder.

Memphis has arrived to get in on the action, but liver is just too precious. Blood, I'm all about the blood. He keeps glaring at me while I eat—the annoying kid begging for candy who doesn't get the message. I lose it and lunge at him, snapping my bloody jaws just at his face.

Mr. Chin yells at me, but I'm already giving Memphis an apology lick. We're still mates; he just can't have my liver!

Problems, I Have Problems

I can't believe Mr. Chin left me untied. He fed me a big slab of beef this morning, but my stomach still feels empty. Doesn't he know there's a flock of sheep in the distance? This is like someone trying to quit cigarettes at a smoky house party. *Yo, mate. Can I have a drag?*

I'm off, full stride. I rocket through the barbed-wire fence, scrape my back, and leave underfur on the middle wire. Sheep lift their heads and waste no time fleeing, but they are too slow. I barrel into the nearest lamb, and it crumples to the ground. I burrow through the wool for a solid bite. In the distance, I hear Mr. Chin, but nothing else matters. My teeth are almost into flesh. A hand whacks me across the head, then those hands drag me by my skin. It's Mr. Chin, angrier than I've ever seen him.

"No! Big Head! No!"

As he drags and whacks me, I yelp. Now he is on his knees, and we are eye to eye.

"No! Bad! You're gonna get shot! Bad!"

I'm half dragged and half whacked back to the van, and I sit as I'm told. Mr. Chin rummages through a bin, pulls out a rope, and knots it at both ends.

After tying me to the hitch, he kneels, cups my face in both hands, and puts his forehead to mine. His voice is gentle now.

"No, boy. No. You can't do that. I don't want to lose you."

Return of the Steak

Mr. Chin tosses a steak at the floor. When it doesn't make a loud enough slap, he picks it up and whips it again. These are the types of things a man can do when he lives by himself with a dog—throw raw meat around the kitchen. Actually, Mr. Chin would probably still do that stuff if he lived with a girl, because he doesn't give a crap. My kind of guy.

I lick at the first landing place. It's amazing how much flavor can transfer in a single slap of meat. When the spot tastes like regular ol' floor again, I get to work on the steak, gnawing and dropping it a few times. Once it's positioned right, it folds in my mouth and slides down in one gulp. I'm used to tearing smaller and rounder pieces of meat fresh off a carcass. These flat slabs take a little getting used to. You'd never find a uniform one-inch-thick slab of meat in the wild. After I lick the last of the flavor off my paws and lips, I follow Mr. Chin outside.

He cleans and packs the van as he tells me we're going on a big road trip. Today the van is parked in its normal spot in front of the door. I heard him talking with a neighbor about how he parks it in a defensive position when the Black Power and Mongrel Mob are fighting. Our house lies on the main road, and apparently some guys think it's tough to randomly shoot at houses. So Mr. Chin tucks the van up under the eaves to block the front window. The van is brilliant and efficient bulletproofing.

I heard someone ask Mr. Chin, "Bet you didn't think you'd have to worry about a drive-by living here, eh, Mr. Chin?"

"Yeah. If a bullet goes through both sides of the van and the front wall of the house and still gets me, then I reckon it's my time," replied Mr. Chin with a chuckle.

Return of the Steak

As I stated before, not much fazes Mr. Chin anymore. At the moment though, he stops everything to acknowledge the guttural noises trumpeting out of my mouth. His eyes widen as my breathing sputters and I stagger along convulsing. Was that steak still alive? Why is it trying to come back out? Mr. Chin kneels as if he hopes to cough it up for me. After much effort and encouragement from Mr. Chin, the steak escapes my body. It hits the ground in a bunch then flattens out into the exact same shape that it went down.

Mr. Chin scoops it up and mutters something about it not being natural. I butt up against his hand, telling him I'll give it another go, but he ignores me and disappears into the house. To my delight, he returns in a minute with the meat nicely cubed in a bowl. I should know to trust this guy by now.

Country Boys

Cars whizz by, Mr. Chin tells me to sit, and we wait for the light to turn green. We cross the street by the dozens. Women wobble along in colorful shoes that make them taller. When they click by, I catch the faint smell of cows in those shoes, and I have to control myself from chewing on them. And I wonder, how can they possibly chase goats in those shoes?

Storefronts extend in both directions as far as I can see. I can't find a tree or a fence post, so I stop at a fire hydrant. Judging by the stained paint and surrounding concrete, hydrants are the preferred marking spots here in Wellington, New Zealand's capital. Over and over I stop to lift my leg at each hydrant. To all dogs in the big city: Big Head is here!

The Big Head Diaries

The dogs here are different. Small fuzzy dogs with crazy haircuts that smell like human soap and flowers prance down the sidewalks. We look at each other and raise our noses, examine each other as though we are foreigners, and I wonder if they think I smell like shit.

While I've been washed two times in my entire life, these little dogs with poofy haircuts probably have a bath once a week. Their moms and dads spend more on their grooming in a month than families spend on food.

I'm sure they'd be afraid to crash through stagnant puddles stained with sheep droppings, and they'd turn their heads from blood. They'd freeze at the sight of a big billy goat instead of circling, waiting for an opening. Would they even know what to do with a roasted lamb tail? Would they know how to stand a bone on end and gnaw through to the marrow?

We shuffle along with the herd and weave through the crowds. Occasionally, Mr. Chin ties me up and goes into a store. No logs to kill, and I can't dig in concrete. What the hell am I supposed to do? I lunge and bark and rear up on my hind legs. People laugh as they walk by. Hopefully this will speed up Mr. Chin's shopping. I don't mean to sound selfish, but a trendy shirt could easily be worth a dozen steaks. We need to keep our priorities in line.

"You look great with the shirt on your back. Now let's go to the butcher's!"

Country Boys

As I bark at Mr. Chin through a window, a cocker spaniel seizes my attention. She looks back over her shoulder with dark, glassy eyes. She holds her gaze until she disappears into the crowds, obviously enamored with Big Head, a country boy in the big city.

Her scents linger, or maybe I *want* her scents to linger. I bark at her. Nothing vulgar. Just a "hello may I smell your privates please" kind of bark. When she doesn't reciprocate, I lunge in her direction and rear up on my hind legs. Mr. Chin comes out with a few bags, unties me, and calls me a nut.

We turn the opposite way of the cocker spaniel, but luckily ladies abound: furry and nonfurry. Mr. Chin knows this too: his neck cranes; his gait slows and quickens. I do my stinky part looking up at the pretty ones, and Mr. Chin slows down to allow them to pet me. Maybe I reek, or maybe he needs to talk a bit more instead of just standing around smiling, because nothing eventful happens.

Today we are both dogs on the prowl in the big city. If we don't score, that's okay. In a few days we'll be back on the open road, ocean out our window, the sun shooting spears of light through waving tree branches. We might not have ladies in our lives, but we have each other, and that's more than enough.

Dad

The incoming tide extends the reach of the ocean, bit by bit. Foaming chaos recedes, leaving saturated sand, rock, and wood, a montage of Earth's building blocks. I chase Mr. Chin down the beach; our prints set and disappear with the lapping waves. The sand is our canvas. I have one wish: that we will leave a trail on the other side of the Pacific. Two weeks on the road cemented our bond.

Mr. Chin is Dad.

We race down the beach, sea spray covering our legs. We swirl, swerve, and spin our way back to Lonna. At the campsite, I settle in to watch Dad cook. My hind legs stick straight out like a human in a recliner. Sand spatters dot my face, and water drips from the edges of my jaw.

"C'mon, mate. Brekki ready or what?" I jibe.

"Dude. You know how good your life is now? Fresh eggs, bacon, and potatoes cooked up on the beach. What a life! Big Head! Big Head! Big Head is a good boy!"

Dad is especially stoked because he surfed this morning. We rocked up late last night and walked to the edge of the ocean, unable to see into the dark. Dad slugged his beer and smiled. "Winds are offshore. Sounds big. Could be pumping in the morning!"

I responded with a yawn and wondered, *Where's the beef?*

That's the thing with surf. The winds, the tide, the swell size, and the swell direction all have to come together for Dad. My stoking activities aren't as complicated. I see a log. I kill it. I find a decaying marine mammal. I slurp away. I see sheep. I chase. It's as simple as that.

When we woke this morning, it was as Dad predicted. Long lines of waves as tall as the van peeled along the beach with no one in sight. The dawn light pushed through the cresting energy, and rainbows danced in

Dad

the spray. Dad squeezed into his wetsuit, let out a hoot, and ran like a kid bursting onto the schoolyard at recess.

At first I killed a few logs, dug a few holes, and hunted for rotting blubber, but after watching Dad race down the line of a wave, I wanted in on the fun. I leaped over the whitewash over and over and stuffed my body through the pounding waves.

When I popped out the back of the break zone, Dad looked at me and said, "Big Head! What the hell, boyeeeeee!"

Like a cat who suddenly finds itself high in the treetops, it hit me. What was I doing? I would have made a tasty snack for a shark. The waves were so big the beach disappeared as they broke. Dad saw my panicked, bulging eyes and paddled over. He grabbed my collar and the scruff of my neck and pointed us toward shore. The ocean tossed and tumbled us, depositing two hungry souls onto the beach. Now, breakfast can't come soon enough.

As I sit and watch Dad chop, stir, and fry, I wonder what America is like. Are there goats, pigs, and sheep? How will we get there? Is he taking me with? Is he allowed to take me?

Questions. I have questions but no answers right now, just the sun drying my fur, sand falling away, the glistening of the sun on the ocean, and my dad beside me.

My dad. I have a dad.

The bacon is a nice touch too.

Hangaroa Trip

Sheep scatter ahead of us. Every time I veer off to chase one, a herding dog cuts me off and I hear Dad yell from the back of an ATV. Too many eyes on me to make a kill, so I focus on my speed and stamina. For now I'm an addict turned long-distance athlete. While I run, Dad and his mate bounce along on the back of the ATV.

The Big Head Diaries

We're on our way to the headwaters of the Hangaroa River. Dad hiked the area months earlier during a pig hunt and asked the landowners if he could come back when fishing season opened. He enjoyed the hunt and even gutted a pig, but he's more of an angler.

The river borders a preserve, so it's a stark contrast in terrain. On one side of the river, the hills are green and dotted with sheep; the native bush burned away long ago. On the other side of the river, the land is untouched and full of old-growth, towering trees and ferns so thick it feels like you have to swim through the leaves.

We set up camp at a fork where a large feeder stream enters the Hangaroa. At the tip of the peninsula where the streams meet, logs and trees form a giant pile stacked there by high waters. It appears as though I have a lot of work to do, and I get to it right away, yanking pieces away until I find one of just the right tenderness. The tang on my gums and tongue is missing with the lack of saltwater in the logs. The many logs taunt me. I lose focus and start another log, then another, running back and forth with Dad egging me on. He laughs at me and mumbles something about ADD.

Dad strings up his rod and carefully picks out a fly he tied a few evenings ago. In between naps by the fire, I watched him take pieces of fur and feather and fasten them to a hook with thread. It seems like a lot of trouble to catch a fish, but taking things to artistic levels is something I've come to admire about humans.

Hangaroa Trip

Whatever. I just hope he catches something and dishes me the scraps. He slips on his waders and strolls over to the river with me following close behind. His eyes squint as he targets tiny seams and bubble lines in the currents. The rod waves back and forth, delivering the fly to its intended mark.

And just like that, he's into a nice rainbow trout. I'm more of a red meat kind of guy, but I'll take anything after that long run. I sniff the air and stare at him, but he ignores me and slips the fish back into the water with a smile. Letting food get away on purpose! This is more proof that humans are nuts.

He does this not once but all day long. I follow him along the bank and cross the water when he crosses. Sometimes I follow behind him, and sometimes I forge ahead or beside him. The river is small here in the headwaters. Like many friendships, rivers start as a trickle and gain power over time. Every drop, every smile, every tear adds to the flow, carving eternal memories.

We ford the river over and over, and each time it feels like we are going somewhere new. The water pushing on our legs, the gurgling of the water as it redirects, and the gravel shifting below our feet remind us that change is constant. It makes me wonder how many streams, rivers, and lakes we will touch in our future.

Exorcism

Dad shuffles along, sneaking in some last-minute fishing as we wait for our ride. This is our final day on the Hangaroa River after four glorious days in the backcountry. We spent our days following the river for long, winding miles, Dad waving a fly rod and me sniffing and hunting for food. I never ventured far, though, as Dad kept an eye on me. He doesn't trust me after the last sheep incident. Even though I'd rather see him killing large game and tossing hunks of meat at me, after all this time I understand why he fly fishes and releases the fish he catches.

It's about the chase.
It's about the smile on our face.
It's about being in a stunning place.

Dad says that trout live in places where water runs cold and clear; this place is one of them. I can only hope Dad and I will visit more. We walk along the river, staying within sight of the pickup point. Dad looks for trout while my stomach growls. He's feeding me a lot, but I'm still famished, like I'm eating for two. I'm a guy. I can't have puppies. It has to be something else.

Even Dad has noticed my leanness, rubbing my ribs, massaging my belly, and examining my poo. All Moms and Dads should look at their dog's crap every now and then and be aware of how much we are eating or not eating. It's one of our only ways to let you know something is wrong.

Dad stops suddenly and tells me to stay. I watch him climb a bank above a deep pool for a better vantage point. Fly fishing for trout is a bit more methodical than sheep hunting. Where I would jump a fence and run full bore at a herd, Dad studies the water, looking for fish, watching their movement, and slinking into a good position to cast. He spots one and slithers back down into a casting position.

As he pulls the line out, I get *the feeling* and hobble away bull-legged. I squat, whimper, and tremor.

Exorcism

Dad notices my condition and scurries up the bank. I'm squeezing, but nothing is coming out. Dad bends down and lifts my tail to investigate.

He leans back and says, "Holy shit, boy!"

I'm not sure what *holy* means in this case, but it's reasonable to assume there are no angels exiting my ass. Out of the corner of my eyes, I see him pulling hand over fist like he's raising a boat anchor. He's gutting me! I want to run, but Dad tells me to stay. I've learned to trust this guy, so I stay, trembling with each pull.

He stands and says it again, "Holy shit, boy!"

He holds up something long and stringy and nearly as tall as him. I rocket away with my rump trying to catch up to the rest of my body. I am free. No wonder I was always hungry. Feeding a tapeworm twice as long as you will do that.

Dad balls it up and tosses it into the stream. We watch it drift away. With Dad's hand on my back, we have a good chuckle about our latest bonding experience. The worm snags on a rock and waves in the current. A strong gust of wind flips my ears back and ripples the water, obscuring the worm from view. Our gaze stays fixed on the spot, and calmness returns in time to see the worm break free. We follow it until it drifts out of sight into a deep pool.

We sigh.

Parasites suck and a river runs through it.

Everything Is Better with Gravy

Dad mutters to his mate Andy, "Big Head will put me in the poorhouse eating fresh meat every day, so this will have to do."

He pulls a pot off the stove and pours a mix of boiled rice and beef onto those horrible pellets. I step forward as he pats me on the head, and I sniff the steaming goodness before he places it on the counter.

"Too hot, buddy. But this is what you get. You can't have pizza every day!"

Dad says something to his mates about how I'd wolf it down and probably burn my tongue and the roof of my

The Big Head Diaries

mouth the same way he used to do that eating pizza in college. I don't know what college is, but I've been around pizza before.

It's actually bullshit, because Dad talks as though he's given me *pizza* before. He's given me crusts with burnt cheese or, if I was lucky, a tiny pepperoni remnant. That's not pizza; that's white bread with flavor accents.

A few more of Dad's mates pop in, and I nose up, smelling at their crotches. Dad yells. His mates yell. I don't know why they are yelling. Their crotches are right here at nose level; you can tell a lot from a crotch sniff. Dad's friends are sweet as.

In between talking about the lack of girls in his life, Dad blows on the steaming bowl and slugs a beer until my food is cool enough to eat. I want to be defiant and refuse the pellets, but I'm hungry, so I nose up to the soupy mess and take a tentative lick. Not bad. I lap away until the broth is mostly gone. By this time the pellets have soaked up the lovely beef flavor, and they slip right down. It's not bloody lamb chops or fatty ribs, and it's nowhere close to the succulence of fresh beef livers, but I'll hand it to Dad—he knows his food. Pellets with gravy I can dig.

Andy looks in the pot and says, "Mate! That looks lovely. Can I have a bowl?"

Dad replies, "I got us covered, bro."

Dad brought a big bag of fish fillets to cook. We caught a mess of fish at the Mohaka River mouth last night, and

Everything Is Better with Gravy

now he's preparing a feast. As I said before, I'm not a huge fan of fish, but now that I'm on the pellets, I'll take anything different. Dad talks of going to the store for mussels. I'm on board with taking a ride, because there is steak at the store.

Before long though more beers open, the room fills with smoke from a bubbling tube, and Dad declares he's not driving anywhere. I'm not sure what they are smoking, but their laughs are contagious. Dad buckles over and has a hard time breathing, his eyes mere slits. I wonder if he can even see. I want in on the fun, so I so attack an empty box. I bark and skid across the kitchen floor, shaking the box in my teeth.

Dad and his mates yell, but this time they encourage me instead of telling me to stop.

"Get it, boy!"

"Kill that thing!"

"You show that box!"

The tearing sound and the cheers send me into a frenzy; I am the center of attention! One dude kicks at the box, and I bark. Dad rolls up a large piece of cardboard and slaps me across my head. I lunge at the makeshift club in his hand, but Dad parries my snout with the cardboard club and catches my cheek with his other hand. He works me over and reaches for my leg. Damn dude has a black belt in dog wrestling. Soon there is no choice but to surrender my belly.

"Mate! Big Head is sweet as!" a man tells Dad.

Dad quickens his belly rub and whispers, "I know. I know..."

A few girls show up. Smiles turn to drop-jawed panting; Dad and his mates jockey for position. And they say we dogs are the animals! Without trying, I seem to be at the top of the head-patting order. Dad could use this to his advantage, but as usual he grins more than he talks.

The good times carry on late into the night. I find a cozy place near the woodstove to keep an eye on the action. No one needs help from me tonight to laugh. In this case I was adding to the happiness—making them smile more. We dogs can be the main course—a human's only source of joy and solace—or we can be the sprinkles on top of ice cream. The fire crackles, my back warms, and I feel hands—those lovely hands.

Shocked

We rock up to our usual spot on a grassy flat, the Mohaka River winding along beyond a wire fence. Dad jumps out and rips open the door. Instead of charging out, I step out, never taking my eyes off the fence. I sit firmly, a boxer in his corner staring down his opponent. Dad smirks and runs off, stepping over the single wire. Pointing the video camera in my direction, he yells for me to come.

The heavy, late-season rains delivered a new influx of driftwood and pumice for Dad to collect along the riverbank. He's taking a suitcase of pumice home with him, so we've been coming here for days.

Yesterday the fence sent shock waves through me, thus

my hesitation to join Dad right now. To join him I must pass the fence! He turns his back to me and walks away.

"Big Head! Big Head! Big Head!" he chants over his shoulder.

Staying close to the van, I wonder if the fence received orders to destroy me. Have the goats and sheep summoned an invisible demon to seek retribution for my reign of terror? Dad turns and shows no concern of my hesitancy. In fact, he's laughing and alternating between looking at me through the video camera's viewfinder and staring me in the eye. The bugger must be in on this trick!

Well, there is only one thing to do. I will show him that nothing stops the Big Head.

I charge, but I have doubts about whether to dive under or jump over the wire. I stop short to eye Dad and the fence. Retreating, I notice the bottom gap is bigger with the dropping slope to the river's edge. Now all I need is speed. My ears flap back; I'm a full-on missile. I stretch my legs in opposite directions; my belly skims the ground. Just like that, I'm through to the other side.

Head down and straight into the things that cause pain—that's how you get 'er done, mate! One cannot run from their fears. If I had a middle finger, I'd use it. Instead, I pounce on a log at the river's edge.

Getting Soft

When Dad ties the rope on, he tells me it's for my own good. I know I can chew through the flimsy rope, but I enjoy pleasing Dad. Must be getting soft. Besides, being tied to the van isn't bad. I can take shelter under the van or inside, because Dad leaves the back hatch open for me. Sometimes Memphis joins me inside the back hatch, and we chill all day. We give each other a lick, look out at the horizon, and shoot the shit.

The Big Head Diaries

We talk mostly about food and ladies but not necessarily in that order. Today we talk mostly food.

"Mate, Dad's neighbors gave him a bucket of lamb hearts yesterday," I brag.

"Sweet as. Got any left?"

"Yes. I mean no. Dude, remember what happened with the liver?"

"That's cold, mate, just cold. At least tell me about it."

"Well, they are about the size of a human fist. You'd think that there would be more blood in a heart, but there isn't. Maybe they clean it first. Anyways...yeah. It's sweet as, mate. Chewier than liver. Not as rubbery as tripe."

"Damn. That's perfect. Let's go!"

I growl at the idea; Memphis changes the subject.

"Did you meet the new bull mastiff down the way?"

"No," I reply, turning my attention to the smell of raw meat.

I stand and sniff in an attempt to zero in and spot a group of men carrying large wire baskets and firewood up to the field.

"Forget about the mastiff. They're firing up a hangi!" I say to Memphis.

"That's the one, mate!" barks Memphis as he turns in circles.

Usually, I prefer my lamb raw—unless it's a *hangi*. A hangi is a traditional way of cooking for the Maoris. It's a great way to prepare food for a lot of people.

Getting Soft

The first step for a hangi is to play with matches. Once a fire is roaring, you toss hangi stones into the flames. Hangi stones are a type of volcanic stone that holds extreme heat without exploding. When the stones are hot and the fire reduced to coals, it's time for the food, such as the neighbor's sheep, a road-killed deer, or the mammoth pig you stabbed over the weekend.

Traditionally, the meat was wrapped in leaves, but nowadays aluminum foil and wire baskets are the go-to vessels for housing the food. Alongside the chunks of mammal, you toss in potatoes and *kumara* (Maori sweet potato). Cover it all up quickly with wet burlap, top it with dirt, and kick back with beers until it's time to unearth it. The longer you can allow the heat and steam and earth's sweetness to permeate the meat, the better.

When it's uncovered, the meat falls away from the bones, and there is more than enough for everyone. Bones are discarded, food is dropped, and I do my job of not allowing anything to go to waste. When a hangi is on, *it's on!*

Memphis turns to me and asks, "Mate, you want me to help you chew through this rope?"

"No, mate. That'll piss Dad off. Dad will let me loose for the hangi. I'm sure of it," I reply.

"No rope chewing? What's happened to you?" he says, shaking his head in mock disappointment. "You've changed."

Grooving

My paws hold a rib bone the same way a possum holds an apple. I nibble at the ends, savoring those bits of bone with fat on the outside and succulent marrow on the inside. Fine cuisine is often about the layers—how different flavors and textures pop as you consume.

Dad points his video camera at me and says, "Dude. You. My friend. Are officially spoiled."

He's got a point. Just a few months ago, I was tied to a chain, cold and hungry. Now, I have an entire box of beef ribs in front of me. Last night I slept inside a house in front of a fire, and I have a dad willing to yank worms out of my ass. I guess that's spoiled, but at least I'm not rotten. Well, sometimes I smell rotten depending on what I've been eating.

Dad turns his attention to Baetis, who's squeezing out from under the house. She looks larger than usual, her belly almost dragging the ground. She doesn't hiss at me anymore, and I keep to myself. Fighting over Dad isn't worth it. He has plenty of love to go around, although if he tries giving her a rib bone, I might growl a little. Just to be sure, I rest a paw on *my* box of ribs.

Sometimes Dad roasts an entire chicken, and we all sit down to dinner in the living room. Dad has stumps in the living room for seats and tables—another thing a man can do when he is single, in addition to tossing raw meat around the kitchen.

He places the steaming chicken on a stump and sits on another stump. Baetis and I join him on either side. He peels hunks of juicy meat off the carcass, waving and blowing on our dinner. When the meat cools, he evenly distributes the goodness. Stomachs full, we settle into our sleeping arrangements, and the night flickers away.

It feels too harmonious. Things are bound to change.

Beach Night

Dad pulls the van tight to the house under the eaves, into defensive position. At a neighbor's house, men in black hoodies stack tires against a corrugated metal fence for bulletproofing. We hurry into our kitchen, and Dad fidgets around, pours food for Baetis and her new kittens, and fills water jugs.

Just when it seemed like Baetis and I started to jibe, she gave birth to kittens. Now she's not just a cat; she's a momma—a tiger. Dad checks on the kittens and gives each of them gentle head rubs. Baetis digs the head rubs most because she was hit by a truck months ago. Both of her rear hips and several ribs were broken, so she is still protective of those areas.

Her kittens, one ginger and one tabby, are tiny whimpering fur balls right now and attached to Baetis more often than not. The ginger kitty looks a little weird, like something isn't quite right. Her head seems too big for her body, and she wobbles when she walks. Dad gives her a few extra head rubs before walking to the van with an armload of gear.

After checking the doors, Dad loads me back into the van and says, "We better sleep at the beach tonight."

The gangs are back at it. This time it was a giant brawl with one man killed. Another man was stabbed and is now in a coma. Once again, Dad is concerned we may be in the line of fire, so we'll be staying oceanside tonight. I was looking forward to curling up on the rug by the fire, but I'm not going to protest a trip to the beach.

Dad stops and waves at a man standing guard at a neighbor's house. Teenagers wearing blue hoodies stack tires against the corrugated metal fence to fortify their positions. Dad chuckles and tells the man we are sleeping at the beach. The man gives us a clenched-fist salute, the sign for the Black Power; he is protecting the family of one of Dad's students. We chug on past the house and out of town, and I catch a glimpse of the man cinching down his hood.

By now I know I can catch a short nap on the way to the beach. The final steep downgrade that takes us onto the sand is my cue to wake up. So once we accelerate out

Beach Night

of town, I do a few turns in the passenger seat and settle in for a power nap.

I stir when Dad stops and shifts the van into four-wheel drive. Dropping down to the beach, the sound of the pounding waves creeps in, and our tires crunch the flotsam just above the high tide line. I stand at attention and wait for my cue.

Dad turns to me and pretends to talk into a radio: "At the drop point—inserting Big Head—out!" He rolls down the window, leans his seat back, and yells, "Go, boy! Go!"

I bound across his lap and leap out the window. The van's tires spin as my paws hit the sand, and the race is on. As usual my initial burst and superb traction send me into a brief lead, but alas, an animal is no match for the combustion engine, and Dad overtakes me. I fall in behind the van and sprint dead center between the tire tracks. Our tracks are the only ones on the beach leading to a grouping of large logs, our camp for the night. As I run up, I hear Dad radio base that we are in position and ready for our next orders.

He opens the back hatch and asks, "Round eighty-eight, boy?"

He should know by now there's no need to ask. I'm always ready to throw down. We've engaged in epic boxing matches, wrestling, tugs-of-war, and now this—a stick fight! He snatches a stick that he uses to mount his camera. I've heard him call it an organic monopod.

The Big Head Diaries

Backpedaling and holding the stick from the middle, he pokes and prods with both ends.

Slow and drawn-out *wahhhhhhh* and *hi-yahhhhhhhh* sounds reverberate from his throat, a Chinese man's version of a growl.

I lunge at his body, crowding him and pushing the pace. If I stay tight, I jam his movements. Dad swivels, spins, and shifts, creating space to catch me in the belly and across the face. I time the next swipe and latch onto the end, lock my legs, and pull Dad to the ground. He laughs and lets go. This round goes to Big Head!

After a head rub, he wanders off to collect kindling for a fire. I notice movement on the hillside and sniff at the air. My stomach grumbles. I slink away, stopping to mark a few logs. I can't seem like I'm in too much of a hurry or Dad may notice. He's on his knees, breaking small sticks and dropping them onto a pile of dried grass.

The sun drops behind the hills, barely reaching out to the eastern horizon over the ocean. Dad calls this the magic hour when he fishes for trout. This is the magic hour for me too. Those are lambs on the hillside, and it's been hours since I've eaten. They look tastier than usual, silhouetted against the fading light.

I reach the base of the hill and glance back. Dad blows at the base of a small fire. Smoke rises, and he watches it dissipate into the skies, seemingly lost in thought. I heard him talking with Angie about the gang

Beach Night

culture and the violence and how he's striving to understand it.

I stare too long and he yells for me. The breeze shifts, and I catch a faint whiff of sausages. I turn to the hillside and he yells again. In between the sound of waves, I hear the meat sizzling.

Fresh lamb, or sausages by the fire with Dad? When did life become so wrought with tough decisions? With my tail windmilling, I trot back to the fire and am greeted with head rubs. I'll have lamb for breakfast.

With our bellies full, Dad kicks back as darkness arrives. I snuggle up beside his chair, within easy reach of his hand. We stare out at the blackness, a wave crashes, and sheep baa in the distance.

The Kill

The sun rises over the ocean. The instant heat warms my ass and back as I dart up a hillside. I don't hear Dad, and even if I did, I wouldn't look back. Last night I let these sheep off, but this morning fresh food is on the menu. Breakfast is literally calling me.

Bahhhhhhhhhhh!

My pace quickens. I crest the hill and am greeted with a flock of chops. In between the sound of the ocean waves and the sheep's frantic baas, I hear Dad yell. He knows what I'm about to do! I can't help it. Like a true addict, I continue my destructive behavior against the wishes of loved ones.

The sheep turn and run, but they are too slow. I choose the nearest and slowest target and drag the struggling meal to the ground. The wool is thick, but my teeth find the mark; blood is everywhere. This is not a game; this is the real deal. The sheep fights and kicks for its life. My jaws stay tight and soon it is over. The immediate loss of heat surprises me. Even through the thick wool, I feel the body lose its warmth.

I grunt and pull on the sheep's neck, shredding the wool away and searching for a clean bite of skin and flesh. Then I feel him before I hear him. Dad holds my face to the ground, picks me up by my skin, and flings me away. He checks the sheep's neck and touches its chest.

"Yeah, Dad. She's dead all right."

"Big Head! Bad boy, bad boy!" he yells. "You're going to get killed!"

He holds the scruff of my neck the entire way down to the van, stopping to scold me a few times. I have nothing to say. I truly have a problem.

I hunker down in the back of the van as Dad shouts obscenities at me. I hate upsetting Dad, but damn—it's not my fault. I've been fed real food with real blood all my life.

Dad stops by a few of the houses near the beach to see if anyone is around. He wants to pay for the sheep I killed. No one is home, and that's good. They'd probably insist on killing me. If I get caught in the act, I'm as good as dead.

Dad doesn't know if he'll be allowed to take me back to America. I think he's been afraid to ask if I'm simply a

The Kill

dog on loan to him or if we can be together forever. I hope he finds out soon. If I stay here, I'm sure to die.

After a long stretch of silence, he turns to me, and with a slight grin he says, "Do you know what you've done? Now I'm harboring a fugitive! Big Head…Big Head. You. My friend. Are a nut!"

Short but Fun

Dad has his tail between his legs. Tears fill his eyes as he cradles the ginger kitten. He sets her down, strokes her oversized head, and hopes she will walk. Her weak legs will not lift her body. Baetis licks the ginger kitten and meows. The tabby kitten is off in the corner chasing ghosts, unaware that his sister is leaving us.

I overheard Dad talking about the kitten and his old dog. Dad told Angie that when his old dog couldn't have fun anymore, then he knew it was time. His dog developed liver disease and slowly grew weaker over a few months until it was time to give his dog lasting peace. I also learned Dad's brother died from cancer.

The Big Head Diaries

Dad knew this day would come soon for the kitten. It was easy to see something wasn't quite right from the day she was born.

We walk out to the van past the crimson stalks of chard where she played weeks ago, unaware her life would end soon. Although I did not play with the ginger kitten, she spent a lot of time in the garden, stalking her tabby brother and chasing her mom's tail. Her life was short, but at least she lived long enough to have fun.

Dad tells me to get in the van, and we take off together with the ginger kitten in a small box. We make the somber ride into town and drop the kitten off at the vet. When Dad gets back in the van, he puts his hand on my head and kneads my forehead as he drives.

"You're coming back with me, boy. You and Baetis are going to America," he says, his voice lowering to a whisper, "I hope."

When the school year is over, he'll leave for America. What will happen then? I lift my head off the car seat and stare at Dad, the passing headlights illuminating his face. He's smiling, but I also see tears in his eyes.

Good Morning

Dad runs and grabs the edge of the school's roof. His body swings forward, and on the backswing he throws his legs over the edge. Balls stop on the playground, kids halt in their tracks, and I pause midstride.

He disappears toward the center of the roof. Kids tiptoe and jump to follow his movements until he is out of sight. Possums have invaded the school's attic, so Dad set traps on the roof. They've eluded him a few times—stealing the bait one night and completely ignoring the traps another night. Maybe today is the day. Fresh possum for breakfast sounds good to me.

"We got one!" he yells.

A collective cheer fills the air. I bark and rear up on my hind legs to join in the celebration. Dad walks to the edge of the roof and windmills the carcass into the air as part of the show. It hits the ground with a thud, and Dad swings down to high-five some of the boys.

"The trail of apples got 'em!" he says.

Dad talks about making a hat, and an older boy offers to help him skin it after school. He slips it into a bag and sets it on the front seat of the van.

He rubs my head and says, "Promise you'll get the meat after we skin it, but you can't have it now."

Dad leaves me off leash, as there's still time before school starts. I consider dragging the bagged possum into the bushes when Dad isn't looking but decide to scavenge the schoolyard instead.

The kids return to their morning business, shedding their jackets, and their dew footprints in the grass disappear with the morning sun. I make my rounds on the schoolyard, checking the bushes, rounding the rubbish bin, and hoping for another slab of pâté. No such luck.

Then there is yelling. Kids on the play structure tiptoe. Their heads turn in unison as though they're following something. Dad rushes out the classroom door and runs to the structure.

A man on an ATV streaks by, and then I see the horses. Horses bolt across the field. One horse stops to buck. Lines of muscles crease through its skin, its mane

Good Morning

following the flowing movement. We freeze, mesmerized by the power.

The older boys bolt by me. They are the Loose Stock Response Team. Earlier in the year, the boys and Dad helped round up a half dozen cows. As the last of the team passes me, I figure what the hell and join in the chase. What will I do when I catch up to an animal twenty times the size of me? I have no idea, but as they say—go hard or go home, mate!

"No. Hey! Come here, boy!" yells Dad.

Like a runaway truck, there is no stopping me now. My muscles pulse, and the wind pushes my ears back and dries my flapping tongue. Even if it will not end in a bloody meal, chasing big game is my game.

The horses find a hole in the fence and curl over a hill. Dad snaps my collar on and leads me back to the van and the possum. He rubs my head and smiles.

"You are truly a fricken nut!" he says as he walks off.

After such an exciting morning, there's nothing to do but bed down in the shade of the van—a napping nut dreaming of fresh possum.

Fishing with Tim

We grind up a steep driveway. I catch a whiff of goodness and perk up like a kid who walks into a bakery that has fresh cookies. I push my nose out the window, and then I see it—a giant pile of freshly skinned Australian possums. I spin in my seat; Dad laughs and pats my head.

"Hold on, boy. We'll get you one," he says.

One! Just one! Look at the pile...

The carcasses are at least ten deep, smooth and succulent. Luckily for me, people hunt Australian possums around here for fur. The possums, like any mammal in New Zealand besides bats and marine mammals, are nonnative. Deer, goats, rats, pigs, cats, possums, stoats, and rabbits were all introduced. All of them have a negative impact on the native plants and bird species. The flightless kiwi, New Zealand's national bird, is impacted greatly, so one doesn't have to feel bad nailing a hundred possums in one night.

So severe is the problem that a man from the government recently visited the school and passed out "Possum Buster" stickers to the kids. There is a bounty on their pelts, making it even more rewarding.

The possums are nocturnal with large eyes, so they're an easy target to spotlight at night. Shooting them is fast and humane, but bullets cost money. Kids often use clubs to kill them, which is messy but effective. Between catching and selling wild goats and hunting possums, a kid around here could theoretically fund their higher education by helping rid the country of invasive species.

Even Dad gave possum hunting a try during winter. Taking a break from writing by the fire, he'd slink around to the back of the house where a couple of orange trees grow on the property. Lacking the acrobatics of a squirrel and aggressiveness of a raccoon, possums are fairly easy prey for a Chinese man with a spear who needs relief from cabin fever. No bars where we live. No movie theaters. Dad doesn't have a girlfriend. What else should a man do at ten o'clock on a Friday night?

We're at Tim's house; he's one of Dad's fishing buddies. He's only eleven years old, but Dad has never treated

Fishing with Tim

him like a kid. He's simply a fishing mate, there to share in the joys of landing a big fish and there to laugh when Dad slips and falls in the river.

Dad tosses me a possum as he talks to Tim. As I dig in, I hear the words *rabbit* and *sandwich*, and my ears perk up. Apparently Tim nailed a few rabbits along with the possums. Tim is a hunter through and through. Wild pigs, ducks, rabbits, and possums—you name it—if it walks or flies, Tim has shot it. He'd probably shoot fish if he could, as fly fishing is a little too tame and delicate for his demeanor. After I'm done eating the possum, we pile into the van, and I sniff at the rabbit sandwiches.

We peel away down the driveway, the pile of possums obscured by a cloud of dust. One...just one...I can't believe all I got was one! But soon we're opening and closing stock gates then rumbling through rolling hills of green and scattering herds of sheep.

Dad skids to a stop, and we spill out. I stay close to Tim and the rabbit sandwiches. We stumble down a steep trail, and the familiar sound of flowing water fills the air. From this vantage point, I see multiple logjams to target. I lift my snout at a faint scent of goat from downstream and lick my nose. It's just another day on another river with Dad.

Everybody on the Bed

Dad invites me to join him and Baetis on the bed. I was perfectly happy on the floor using a dustpan as a pillow, but I'm not about to ignore an upgrade. Baetis glares at me as I cross the room, her eyes like a scope on a rifle. Dad strokes her head and tells her I'm cool. I try not to make eye contact as I place a paw on the bed; I'm living it up while I can. Who knows what will happen when Dad leaves? First I was allowed inside the house, then on a soft rug in front of a fire, and now in a real human bed. Not bad for a dude who was tied to a tree months ago.

I ignore Baetis and the tabby kitten, turn my back to them, and settle in. It's best not to make a big deal of it, and I'm tired.

Soon my lower lip flops open, and my upper lip flaps as I snore and kick and dream about flocks of skinned lambs stuck in place. Buckets of livers drenched in blood surround me. My stomach is so full I need to shift positions; I wake, turn, and stretch, forgetting that I am on the bed.

Baetis looses her wrath in the darkness, claws raging. Dad is caught in the friendly fire and jumps up. He scolds both of us, and we slink to opposite sides of the room. It's the middle of the night, so he curls back up in bed. I'm not sure who goes first, but we both end up on either side of him again, opting to be close to Dad instead of fighting.

Connection

The kids file onto the rugby field. Beaded skirts click and sway. Some of the boys have face tattoos drawn on called *moko*. They turn to each other and practice their *pūkanas*, an expression of pride often meant to instill fear. Dad circles the group while snapping pictures.

I circle too, but I'm following a stout lady eating a sandwich. A chunk falls away, and I lap up the white bread smothered with butter and savor the small bits

The Big Head Diaries

of ham and cheese. I could do without the white bread, but damn—that butter is lovely. Maybe one day Dad will give me an entire stick of butter. One can always dream.

The children are in position now with the adults facing them. This is the last dress rehearsal for the upcoming haka festivals. The haka, as I mentioned before, is a traditional song and dance taken seriously around here. It's an iconic part of the Maori culture.

In addition to the smells of freshly mowed grass, sheep, and the occasional cigarette, I catch a whiff of the ocean and decaying marine mammal. The kids from our school teamed up with another school for the performance, so we're visiting their school. Their school site sits atop a plateau above the ocean, and my guess is that we'll hit the beach after the rehearsal is done. The thought of an aged-blubber snack gives me something to look forward to.

After last-minute directions and encouragement, silence falls over the field. Even the normal chorus of sheep and cows has ceased. The kids have practiced for months; they demand our attention.

Humans stroke their beards, play with their hair, and twiddle their thumbs to occupy themselves during a show. I don't have a beard or hands or thumbs, so I slump to my side and lick away at my goods. Perfect.

A tall, dark-haired boy stamps and breaks the silence and bellows the first lines of the haka. He waves a replica

Connection

of a Maori weapon, his voice coming from a place much deeper than his throat. For many of the children, they don't just live here, this is *their* land—they are connected. Their ancestors bellowed the haka and stared down enemies with pūkanas where they now stand.

The rest of the group responds. They pound and scratch their chests in unison. Dad whispers to an elderly lady about how lucky he is to witness the haka and how thankful he is to be a part of the community. I don't know what the lady says in return, but she places her hand on Dad's shoulder and smiles. Her gray hair flows in the breeze, eyes squinting into the sun; she joins in the call and response. Soon everyone joins in. The expressions on the kids' faces are beyond their years—powered by long bloodlines.

Applause waves over the field as the kids finish up. Most of the boys scratched their bare chests so hard they are bleeding; I'm sure it gives them bragging rights. They file into a classroom to change into street clothes.

The boys settle back into the present, sporting their gravity-defying baggy pants and bantering about American rappers. And finally the moment I've been waiting for—they spread out in the grass and playground to eat lunch.

I'm up and ready, on the lookout but not begging. They must have worked up an appetite, because the scraps are few and far between. Unfamiliar dogs circle

The Big Head Diaries

with the same idea, some of them quite big, so I am down in the pecking order. Usually Dad has to work after lunch, but school is over for today, and just as I expected, we hop in the van to hit the beach.

As we roll out, Dad turns to me. "You know, boy, this doesn't seem real. Those kids. The haka. You. Baetis and her kittens. And this!" he yells, pumping his fist out the window at the ocean's horizon.

Then he adds, "Hell yeah!"

After the haka I feel stoked too; however, one thing I'd add is the fact there is a strong smell of ripe blubber wafting through the open windows. Toss in a deserted beach, and it's no wonder we're both at the edge of our seats, ready to explode out of the van.

We grind to a stop, and Dad grabs a pair of leather gloves off the dashboard. I circle in my seat, ready for battle, then leap over the gearshift and follow Dad out the door. My weight catches his heels, and we both tumble. Up in an instant, we run to a grassy patch and square off. He catches me with a right hook and a left uppercut, but it has no effect. My big head gives me a good chin.

We circle, look for openings, and pick our shots. I lunge at his fists and at his feet, but he sidesteps and lands a left hook. I growl louder with each blow to my cheeks. My paws rip the air until I find Dad's arm, and I snap at his gloved hands. Dad stops his punching, grabs my cheeks, and drags me to the ground. Those damn

Connection

hands of his give him such an advantage, but there is no shame being submitted by a belly rub. This round goes to Dad.

Dad sheds his gloves, buries his head into my chest, and rubs behind my ears. I paw at his head, but the ecstasy paralyzes me. We freeze—a still frame of connection. Warm sand works into my fur. I can hear Dad's heart as he listens to mine. A wave crashes, and we roll away ready for another round.

Meat Bananas

I chill on the platform in the van, but the morning sun peeks over the ridge with a vengeance. No gradual warm-up, just instant burn. Within minutes everything is blanketed in blazing heat. I heard Dad comment on how he can't get used to Christmastime being in summer and how it feels like his shaved head is on fire. Dad leaves me plenty of slack in the rope, so I hop out and crawl under the van, pawing at the gravel.

A group of kids carries supplies to a storage shed. Dad sloughs chairs from the classroom to the whānau room. *Whānau* is the Maori word for family. The end of school assembly is this afternoon. The start of the four-week summer break is just days away. Kids are moving on to

The Big Head Diaries

high school, and some kids are just starting. Change is everywhere.

It's hard to believe I met Dad here on the schoolyard almost a year ago. That sad face of his when he first saw me is long gone, washed away by sloppy kisses and hundreds of winding miles with me as a copilot.

Just as I start dozing off, I notice a few of the older boys dragging heavy sacks up to the edge of the rugby field. I perk up and sniff the air. When I see them run back for firewood, I know it's on.

Time for lamb tails, or as Dad says, it's time for meat bananas. Whatever you call them, it's one of my favorite snacks. It's docking season around here. The wee little lambs are getting their tails chopped off. Tails get dirty with shit; shit breeds disease. So it's off with the tails!

The heat is forgotten as the delight of lamb tails takes over. Dad unclips me. He knows I won't stray far. He has a huge fire roaring in no time, and the first handfuls of meat bananas hit the grate. The flame burns the crap and the hair away, leaving a charred tail behind. Bacteria cannot survive the inferno. You know it's the proper temperature when you hear a rapid hissing.

When clothes and fur are permeated with the smell of burning hair and the hissing slows, one can consider the meat banana al dente. Eager hands juggle the hot mess and peel away the charred skin to reveal the ghostly white, fatty vertebrae. The kids squeeze lemon juice and

Meat Bananas

pour salt on the steaming delicacy before sucking the fat off. The remaining bones still have plenty of flavor, and I make quick work of the discarded pieces. Crunching down on the soft bones, I wonder if I'd still get shot if I just bit the tails off lambs. I'd be helping, after all, and there'd be no killing involved. The problem is I wouldn't be able to stop at the tail. Probably for the best if I don't touch lambs at all.

Memphis shuffles along with a half dozen other dogs. There's plenty to go around, but Dad still sneaks them straight to me. He laughs with the kids, sucks on a tail, and comments on how he wished for a bowl of his grandpa's special sauce.

Earlier in the year, he whipped up a soy sauce, ginger, and scallion mixture for a lamb-tail roast, adding an Asian flair to this country ritual. Apparently, eating lamb tails is similar to eating chicken feet, something Dad does at a meal called *dim sum*. I wonder if dim sum has lamb? Bet I'd be down with dim sum.

Dad runs the tail through his lips and slurps the very end before holding it up to the sky.

"Sweet as," he exclaims before he flips it at me.

I munch it down. The blue skies, the endless horizons—I'd miss this place, but I'd miss Dad even more if he didn't bring me back to the US. He's leaving soon.

Coming to America!

Dad wrestles a huge stump out of the van. The suspension creaks as it tumbles to the ground. He grunts and rolls it forward, repeating the process over and over, his grunts more melodic and rhythmic with each cycle.

"Sound effects, boy. Sound effects. Sometimes it's all about the sound effects."

He's right. Killing logs without growling and barking isn't nearly as effective.

Normally I prefer killing rotten logs. The soft exterior leading to the intact wood at the log's core makes me feel like a beast tearing apart prey. This stump is a well preserved hardwood, different than what I'm used to, but as we Kiwis say, I'll give it a go, mate!

The Big Head Diaries

I throw my paws against it with all my might, lunging and picking at the knots. This piece would take me years to kill. It's a native hardwood carried from headwater streams to the oceans. Long bands of different colored grains make this one unique. A few teeth marks will only add to its charm.

I bark and snarl louder and louder, my grinding teeth barely making scratches in the wood. Dad laughs and pushes me away. I push back, but he swats me away.

"Down, boy!" he says as he leads me to the last of some livers.

Perfect. Getting my ass kicked by an old stump worked up an appetite.

Dad works on a sculpture using pumice stones and driftwood. His time in New Zealand transformed him in many ways. Not only did he confront his sadness from the loss of his first dog and a brother, but his creative spirit found wings. He writes, edits video, paints, and carves pumice stone. Small pumice carvings grace the mantel, and larger pieces line the front walkway.

Carving is a big part of Maori culture. Their intricate wood and greenstone carvings are renowned. The soft, porous nature of pumice gives immediate gratification, making it a perfect medium for the beginning carver.

This latest piece of driftwood is lighter in color, which adds a nice contrast to the towering sculpture. Once he leans it into place, he leads me back to the van and ties me

Coming to America!

up. The liver is teetering on being too rancid to eat, but the extra juice quenches my log-chewing cotton-mouth. As I chomp away a stock truck whizzes by, leaving a wake of sheep aroma. Dad yells at the driver to slow down.

Not only does he not trust me with the sheep, but he's also been terrified of me being hit by a car since Baetis was hit earlier in the year, a downside to living on a main road.

As Dad walks back to the sculpture, the woman who took me home as a puppy walks up to our fence. Dad looks up at her, his lips pursed. He stays silent with a large piece of pumice in his hands. She can only be here for one reason—to tell him whether or not he can take me back to America.

She leans against the fence and says, "Mr. Chin! We reckon Big Head would be gutted without ya. You should take him."

Dad replies, "You don't know how much that means to me. Maybe I can do something for you guys."

"My yard could use some work. Why don't you make one of these sculptures at my place?"

With the deal done, Dad grabs my cheek and holds his forehead to mine. Baetis charges around the corner of the house, the tabby right on her tail. Dad pumps his fist and screams at the Aotearoa sky, "Big Head! Yeah! Big Head!"

To be continued in
The Big Head Diaries, Volume II.

To see videos of Big Head visit
www.ryanchinauthor.com/big-head-diaries.

A Note from Ryan

Big Head is at my feet as I write this. His snout grows whiter every day, and those damn moles and fatty lumps keep getting bigger and more numerous. He's fourteen years old, and I know that our time is winding down, that every day is a gift.

Volume II is underway. It starts with him stepping foot in the USA and hooking up with an American gal. I let him spread his genes once before I neutered him. I know millions of dogs need a home, but it seemed like the thing to do.

In the meantime, if you need another read, check out *Without Rain There Can Be No Rainbows*. It's my perspective of Big Head and me meeting in New Zealand and a

The Big Head Diaries

lot more. I call it a pet-and-teacher memoir wrapped up into a travel adventure. Electronic versions of *Without Rain* include tightly edited video footage of our time in New Zealand, making it a multimedia experience if you choose. Some of the videos shared in *The Big Head Diaries* are from *Without Rain*.

Thanks for reading.

Ryan Chin

Acknowledgments

I bow in respect to my ancestors who immigrated to the United States. I believe they did what they had to do so that now I can choose what I want to do. I'd like to thank my sister and my mom and dad for the unwavering support of my meandering ways.

To my two amazing kids, Rayden and Jaxen, I hope my writing will inspire you to follow your own creative and expressive paths. You two fill the pages of my life.

To my mate, Brett Neiman, your willingness to create has always inspired me from your college days of picking on corrugated cardboard and filling the grooves with Vaseline to the present day with your music. Thank you for the cover designs on both of my books and for always

The Big Head Diaries

being there. We will produce a movie together some day. I know this to be true.

And to my furry mates past, present, and future, it hurts that your life spans are so short compared to mine, but that leaves the door open for more of you to grace my life. I look forward to the next connection whenever and wherever that may be.

About Ryan Chin

Ryan meanders in Portland, Oregon, and beyond. He's a daddy, home inspector, writer, fly fisher, and a surfer—mostly in that order.

www.ryanchinauthor.com

www.ingramcontent.com/pod-product-compliance
Lightning Source LLC
Chambersburg PA
CBHW020653300426
44112CB00007B/365